SIMPLIFIED ISLAMIC INHERITANCE

An Adapted Elaboration on Mu'īn al-Farā'iḍ

Al Khalil Islamic Academy, publisher
Toronto, Ontario, Canada
publication@alkhalil.ca

ISBN 978-1-7782888-4-5

1st print edition August 2024

بسم الله الرحمن الرحيم

Contents

Foreword

الحمد لله رب العالمين والصلاة والسلام على أشرف الأنبياء والمرسلين محمّد وآله وصحبه أجمعين.

Islamic Inheritance is a unique subject, in the Higher Islamic Studies curriculum, particularly for its focus on abstract concepts. As we were a sisters' class, honoured to be under the tutelage of Mufti Ibrahim Kureshi (ḥafidhahullāh), we found this subject hard to grasp. Oftentimes, without a board or a functional screen projection, we were heavily reliant on the English translation of Mu'īn al-Farā'iḍ and our imagination. The motivation to compose *Simplified Islamic Inheritance* stemmed from our shared experience. The objective was to summarize the concepts and present them in a simplified manner alongside examples provided by our teacher. It is hoped that this edited translation will be conducive to the beginners' learning style and will aid in grasping the intricacies of this science.

Some unique features of this coursebook are:

- Highlighted summaries at the beginning of each lesson
- Numbered lists to illustrate problem-solving steps
- Complete worked out examples

This book was made possible through the efforts of the teachers and students at Al Khalil Academy. With the tawfīq of Allah Ta'āla, we have tried to make this work perfect but as human beings, we have our weaknesses and incapabilities. Thus, we humbly request that you become a part of our concerted effort to make this book a success. If you find any errors or have any suggestions, kindly email us at publication@alkhalil.ca.

Contributors

Sarah Ahmed
Fathima Rasma Mohamed Kamal
Farha Meherdeen
Afrah Mubarak
Saadia Patel
Anam Qudrat
Anjuman Siddiqui

INTRODUCTION

Introductory Principles

Al-Khuḍarī (raḥimahu Allāh) said:

مَبَادِيْ كُلِّ عِلْمٍ كَانَ حَدٌّ ... وَمَوْضُوْعٌ وَ غَايَةٌ مُسْتَمَدٌّ

مَسَائِلُ نِسْبَةٌ وَاسْمٌ وَحُكْمُ ... وَفَضْلٌ وَاضِعٌ عَشَرٌ تُعَدُّ

***Definition* (الحَدّ)**

The principles through which a person learns how to distribute inheritance Islamically.

Linguistically, it means stipulation (*al-taqdīr*) and assignment (*al-taqarrar*) amongst other meanings.

Technically, it refers to knowledge of those principles of *al-fiqh* and *al-hisāb* through which heirs and their rights to the estate are recognized.

***Subject Matter* (الْمَوضُوع)**

The estate of the deceased and the ones deserving it.

***Objective* (الْغَايَة)**

Literally, it means, "end point". It is to know the inheritors, lawful heirs and their due shares.

***Source* (المُسْتَمَد)**

It is taken from the Qurʾān (the verses that specify the *dhawu al-furūḍ*), the Sunnah (which established the *ʿaṣabāt* inheriting) and the Ijmāʿ of the scholars of this Ummah. Qiyāṣ is not used to establish shares, as there is no ambiguity in these rulings.

***Points of Discussion* (المَسَائِل)**

The discussions include the specific heirs, their stipulated and calculated shares. For example, the husband receives half or a quarter of the estate, depending on if he has children.

***Relationship to the other Sciences* (النِّسبَة)**

It is related to Islamic Jurisprudence (*al-fiqh*) and uses basic mathematics (*al-hisāb*).

***Name* (الإسْم)**

ʿIlm al-Farāʾiḍ refers to the Science of Inheritance Distribution. Alternatively, this science is also called *ʿIlm al-Mīrāth*.

***Rank/Status/Importance* (الحُكْم)**

It is a communal obligation (*farḍ kifāyah*). It is sufficient that one or a few individuals have knowledge of this science in a community of Muslims.

***Virtue* (الفَضْل)**

The importance of this science is established by its clear mention in the Quran. Allah says in Sūrah al-Nisāʾ, verses 11-12 and 176:

يُوْصِيْكُمُ اللهُ فِيْٓ اَوْلَادِكُمْۖ لِلذَّكَرِ مِثْلُ حَظِّ الْاُنْثَيَيْنِۚ فَاِنْ كُنَّ نِسَآءً فَوْقَ اثْنَتَيْنِ فَلَهُنَّ ثُلُثَا مَا تَرَكَۚ وَاِنْ كَانَتْ وَاحِدَةً فَلَهَا النِّصْفُؕ
وَلِاَبَوَيْهِ لِكُلِّ وَاحِدٍ مِّنْهُمَا السُّدُسُ مِمَّا تَرَكَ اِنْ كَانَ لَهٗ وَلَدٌۚ فَاِنْ لَّمْ يَكُنْ لَّهٗ وَلَدٌ وَّوَرِثَهٗٓ اَبَوٰهُ فَلِاُمِّهِ الثُّلُثُۚ فَاِنْ كَانَ لَهٗٓ اِخْوَةٌ فَلِاُمِّهِ
السُّدُسُ مِنْ بَعْدِ وَصِيَّةٍ يُّوْصِيْ بِهَآ اَوْ دَيْنٍؕ اٰبَاؤُكُمْ وَاَبْنَاؤُكُمْ لَا تَدْرُوْنَ اَيُّهُمْ اَقْرَبُ لَكُمْ نَفْعًاؕ فَرِيْضَةً مِّنَ اللهِؕ اِنَّ اللهَ كَانَ عَلِيْمًا
حَكِيْمًا (١١)

Allah commands you regarding your children: the share of the male will be twice that of the female. If you leave only two ˹or more˺ females, their share is two-thirds of the estate. But if there is only one female, her share will be one-half. Each parent is entitled to one-sixth if you leave offspring. But if you are childless and your parents are the only heirs, then your mother will receive one-third. But if you leave siblings, then your mother will receive one-sixth—after the fulfillment of bequests and debts. ˹Be fair to˺ your parents and children, as you do not ˹fully˺ know who is more beneficial to you. ˹This is˺ an obligation from Allah. Surely Allah is All-Knowing, All-Wise. (11)

وَلَكُمْ نِصْفُ مَا تَرَكَ اَزْوَاجُكُمْ اِنْ لَّمْ يَكُنْ لَّهُنَّ وَلَدٌۚ فَاِنْ كَانَ لَهُنَّ وَلَدٌ فَلَكُمُ الرُّبُعُ مِمَّا تَرَكْنَ مِنْ بَعْدِ وَصِيَّةٍ يُّوْصِيْنَ بِهَآ اَوْ دَيْنٍؕ
وَلَهُنَّ الرُّبُعُ مِمَّا تَرَكْتُمْ اِنْ لَّمْ يَكُنْ لَّكُمْ وَلَدٌۚ فَاِنْ كَانَ لَكُمْ وَلَدٌ فَلَهُنَّ الثُّمُنُ مِمَّا تَرَكْتُمْ مِّنْ بَعْدِ وَصِيَّةٍ تُوْصُوْنَ بِهَآ اَوْ دَيْنٍؕ وَاِنْ
كَانَ رَجُلٌ يُّوْرَثُ كَلٰلَةً اَوِ امْرَاَةٌ وَّلَهٗٓ اَخٌ اَوْ اُخْتٌ فَلِكُلِّ وَاحِدٍ مِّنْهُمَا السُّدُسُۚ فَاِنْ كَانُوْٓا اَكْثَرَ مِنْ ذٰلِكَ فَهُمْ شُرَكَآءُ فِى الثُّلُثِ مِنْ
بَعْدِ وَصِيَّةٍ يُّوْصٰى بِهَآ اَوْ دَيْنٍۙ غَيْرَ مُضَآرٍّۚ وَصِيَّةً مِّنَ اللهِؕ وَاللهُ عَلِيْمٌ حَلِيْمٌؕ (١٢)

You will inherit half of what your wives leave if they are childless. But if they have children, then ˹your share is˺ one-fourth of the estate—after the fulfillment of bequests and debts. And your wives will inherit one-fourth of what you leave if you are childless. But if you have children, then your wives will receive one-eighth of your estate—after the fulfillment of bequests and debts. And if a man or a woman leaves neither parents nor children but only a brother or a sister ˹from their mother's side˺, they will each inherit one-sixth, but if they are more than one, they ˹all˺ will share one-third of the estate—after the fulfillment of bequests and debts without harm ˹to the heirs˺. ˹This is˺ a commandment from Allah. And Allah is All-Knowing, Most Forbearing. (12)

يَسْتَفْتُونَكَ قُلِ اللهُ يُفْتِيكُمْ فِى الْكَلٰلَةِ اِنِ امْرُؤٌا هَلَكَ لَيْسَ لَهٗ وَلَدٌ وَّلَهٗٓ اُخْتٌ فَلَهَا نِصْفُ مَا تَرَكَ وَهُوَ يَرِثُهَآ اِنْ لَّمْ يَكُنْ لَّهَا وَلَدٌ فَاِنْ كَانَتَا اثْنَتَيْنِ فَلَهُمَا الثُّلُثٰنِ مِمَّا تَرَكَ وَاِنْ كَانُوْٓا اِخْوَةً رِّجَالًا وَّنِسَآءً فَلِلذَّكَرِ مِثْلُ حَظِّ الْاُنْثَيَيْنِ يُبَيِّنُ اللهُ لَكُمْ اَنْ تَضِلُّوْا وَاللهُ بِكُلِّ شَىْءٍ عَلِيْمٌ (١٧٦)

They ask you ˹for a ruling, O Prophet˺. Say, "Allah gives you a ruling regarding those who die without children or parents." If a man dies childless and leaves behind a sister, she will inherit one-half of his estate, whereas her brother will inherit all of her estate if she dies childless. If this person leaves behind two sisters, they together will inherit two-thirds of the estate. But if the deceased leaves male and female siblings, a male's share will be equal to that of two females. Allah makes ˹this˺ clear to you so you do not go astray. And Allah has ˹perfect˺ knowledge of all things. (176)

Furthermore, the Prophet ﷺ emphasized the importance of learning and preserving this science when he ﷺ said:

«تَعَلَّمُوا الفَرائِضَ وعَلِّمُوهُ النّاسَ فَإنَّهُ نِصفُ العِلْمِ وهُوَ أوَّلُ شَيْءٍ يُنْسى وهُوَ أوَّلُ شَيْءٍ يُنْتَزَعُ مِن أُمَّتِي»

"Learn the (knowledge of) inheritance distribution and teach it to the people, for indeed it is half of knowledge. And it is the first of things to be forgotten, and taken away from my nation." (Sunan ibn Mājah, #2719)

«العِلْمُ ثَلاثَةٌ وما سِوى ذَلِكَ فَهُوَ فَضْلٌ: آيَةٌ مُحْكَمَةٌ، أوْ سُنَّةٌ قائِمَةٌ، أوْ فَرِيضَةٌ عادِلَةٌ»

"Knowledge is of three (kinds) and what is besides that, is extra: a clear verse (of the Qurʾān), or an established Sunnah, or a just share (of inheritance)." (Sunan Abū Dawūd, #2885)

***Founder* (الوَاضِع)**

The scholars of *al-ijtihād* gathered this science together. Amongst the Companions, Zayd bin Thābit ؓ was well-versed in this field. The Prophet ﷺ said:

«أَفْرَضُ أُمَّتِي زَيْدُ بْنُ ثَابِتٍ»

"The most (knowledgeable regarding) inheritance from my nation is Zayd bin Thābit ؓ" (al-Istīʾāb, 2/538). The Ṣaḥābah would also say:

«غَلَبَ زَيْدُ بْنُ ثَابِتٍ النَّاسَ عَلَى اثْنَيْنِ: الْقُرْآنُ وَ الْفَرَائِضُ»

"Zayd bin Thābit ؓ overcame the people in two matters: the Qurʾān and the matter of inheritance" (al-Istīʾāb, 2/539).

0.1. Rights due from the Estate (تَرِكَة)

Before the estate of the deceased can be divided amongst the inheritors, there are a few rights that need to be taken care of from the estate. They are mentioned in order below.

1. **Shrouding (التَّكْفِيْن) and Funeral Rites (التَّجْهِيْز)**

   Firstly, the estate will be used for the shrouding and funeral rites of the deceased, even if the entire estate is used up. The shrouding should be moderate in terms of number (three for men and five for women) and value (i.e., what he commonly wears on special occasions like Friday, ʻĪd or meeting relatives).

2. **Debt (الدَّيْن)**

   Secondly, the debts need to be fulfilled, even if the entire estate may be used up. Therefore, any unpaid obligatory alms (*zakāh*) or monetary expiations (*kaffarah*) cannot be given from the estate at this point, unless the deceased included it in his bequest. Debts are of two kinds:

   a. Debt in health (*dayn al-ṣiḥḥah*): It is an established debt (by documentation or two witnesses) that a person incurred in health.

   b. Debt in sickness (*dayn al-maraḍ*): It is a debt that a person incurred in terminal illness and confessed to on his deathbed.

   If the estate cannot cover the amount of debt, then the *dayn al-ṣiḥḥah* will be fulfilled. If the debts are of the same type, the creditors will be paid from the estate proportionate to their respective debts.

3. **Bequest (الْوَصِيَّة)**

   Lastly, the bequest will be fulfilled from up to a third of the remaining estate. The bequest refers to wealth which the deceased stipulated should be given to another, or used for a specific cause. The bequest cannot be for an inheritor. It can also not be used for anything prohibited by legislation.

0.2. Types of Heirs

1. **Inheritors of Stipulated Shares (ذَوُو الْفُرُوْض)**: The primary inheritors with fixed shares from the Qurʾān and Sunnah.
2. **Residuary Inheritors by Lineage (الْعَصَبَات)**: Those heirs who are connected to the deceased through lineage, like the paternal grandfather or grandson. In the presence of the

dhawu al-furūḍ, the *ʿaṣabāt* will receive the remainder of the estate. In their absence, the estate will be divided only amongst the *ʿaṣabāt*.

3. **Residuary Inheritors by Emancipation (مَوْلَى الْعَتَاقَة)**: The master inherits from his freed slave who left behind no inheritors.
4. **Residuary Inheritors of Slave owner (عَصَبَةُ مَوْلَى الْعَتَاقَة)**: If the master of the freed slave has also passed away, then the estate of the freed slave will be inherited by the *ʿaṣabāt* or male relatives of the master.
5. **Redistribution for Lineal Inheritors of Stipulated Shares (الرَّدّ عَلَى ذَوِي الْفُرُوض النَّسَبِيَّة)**: With no *ʿaṣabāt* to inherit the remaining shares, the estate will be redivided amongst the *dhawu al-furūḍ*. The spouses will be excluded from this redistribution.
6. **Maternal Relatives (ذَوُو الْأَرْحَام)**: The inheritors, connected to the deceased through a female, like the maternal grandfather. In the absence of the *dhawu al-furūḍ* and the *ʿaṣabāt*, the *dhawu al-arḥām* will inherit the entire estate.
7. **One who made a contract of Clientage (مَوْلَى الْمَوَالَاة)**: An individual with the contract of clientage (i.e the deceased said to him, "You are my *mawlā*. If I die, you will inherit from me.") will inherit. If the deceased's spouse is present, the *mawlā* will receive the remainder of the estate after the spouse receives their fixed portion.
8. **One whose lineage is confessed (الْمُقَرُّ لَهُ بِالنَّسَب عَلَى الْغَيْر)**: The confession of a family link in which one does not become part of the lineage, like confessing someone is his brother.
9. **Individual Bequeathed the Entire Estate (الْمُوْصَى لَهُ بِجَمِيعِ الْمَال)**: The individual to whom the deceased made a bequest of receiving all of the estate, will be granted the entire estate in the absence of any other inheritor.
10. **State Treasury (بَيْتُ الْمَال)**: In the absence of all the recipients mentioned above, the estate will be taken by the *bayt al-māl*, to be used at the discretion of the Islamic government.
11. **Redivision upon the Spouses (الرَّد عَلَى الزَّوْجَيْن)**: The scholars today have agreed that in the absence of the above recipients, if the deceased is survived by a spouse, the entire estate will be inherited by them.

0.3. Factors that Prevent Inheriting (مَوَانِعُ الْإِرْث)

1. **Slavery (الرِّقّ)**: A slave does not have ownership of himself, thus he cannot have ownership over anything else. This also applies to a slave who has an aspect of freedom attributed to him, like one promised freedom upon the master's death such as the *mudabbar* and *umm al-walad*.

2. **Murder (الْقَتْل):** Murder that necessitates legal retribution (*qiṣāṣ*) or monetary expiation (*kaffārah*) will prevent the murderer from inheriting. Causing a death through any act other than murder will not prevent inheritance. For example, a person dug a ditch and his father who passed by fell into it and died. This will not prevent the one who dug the ditch from inheriting from his father.
3. **Difference of Religion (اخْتِلَاف الدِّيْنِين):** A Muslim will not inherit from a disbeliever (even if he is a relative) and *vice versa*. This is based on the statement of the Prophet ﷺ: "People of two different creeds will never inherit from each other."
4. **Difference of Country (اخْتِلَاف الدَّارَيْن):** Heirs of two different lands (Islamic state (*dār al-ʾislām*) and the land at war with Islamic state (*dār al-ḥarb*)) will not inherit. This difference can be:
    a. In reality (*ḥaqīqah*), meaning one of the individuals is a *dhimmī* (non-Muslim citizen of *dār al-islām*) and the other is a *ḥarbī* (non-Muslim from *dār al-ḥarb*). Since the *dhimmī* is from *dār al-islām* and the *ḥarbī* is from *dār al-ḥarb*, the two cannot inherit from each other.
    b. By decree of law (*ḥukm*), where one individual is a *dhimmī* and the other is a *mustaʾman* (non-Muslim granted safety to visit *dār al-islām* for some time). In reality, the two are in *dār al-ʾislām*, but by decree of the law, the *dhimmī* is protected by *dār al-islām*, unable to return to *dār al-ḥarb* and treated as a Muslim, while the *mustaʾman* will return to *dār al-ḥarb* and is not treated as a Muslim. Therefore, these two will not inherit from each other.
    c. A Muslim living in *dār al-ḥarb* would not inherit from a Muslim living in *dār al-islām* in the case that two non-Muslims (such as a father and son) accept Islam and one of them emigrates to a Muslim country. Further, the other individual dies before he can emigrate. However, in today's context, living in different countries would not prevent Muslims inheriting from each other.
5. **Confusion regarding the heir (جَهَالَةُ تَارِيْخِ الْمَوْتَى)**[1]

    Deprivation from inheritance can occur when there is ambiguity regarding who the heirs are, due to the time or order of deaths being unknown. For example, some family members die simultaneously (i.e. car accidents, natural disasters, etc) and the order of death is not clear. This will prevent the deceased family members from inheriting from each other.

---

[1] A fifth factor is only included according to some.

PART 1: THEORY & FOUNDATION

Chapter 1: Inheritors with Stipulated Shares [ذَوُو الْفُرُوْض]

Dhawu al-furūḍ are those individuals who are entitled to a stipulated share based on the Qur'ān. There are 12 individuals who will receive a stipulated share, four males (father, grandfather, husband, and uterine brother) and eight females (wife, daughter, granddaughter, sister, consanguine sister, uterine sister, mother, grandmother). Their conditions are outlined in Tables 1.1 and 1.2.

Table 1.1. Males with Stipulated Shares

Inheritors[a]	Case	Share	Living relatives of deceased
Father (اب)	I	$\frac{1}{6}$ [b]	has alive, male descendants (i.e., son, grandson, etc.)
	II	$\frac{1}{6}$ + remainder [c]	has alive female descendants (i.e., daughter, granddaughter, etc.)
	III	remainder	has no alive children
Paternal Grandfather (جدّ صحيح)	I	$\frac{1}{6}$	has a son and no father
	II	$\frac{1}{6}$ + remainder	has a daughter or granddaughter and no father
	III	remainder	has no children and no father
	IV	deprived (مَحْجُوْب)	has a father
Husband (زوج)	I	$\frac{1}{2}$	has no children from any marriages
	II	$\frac{1}{4}$	has children
Uterine Siblings (أخياف)	I	$\frac{1}{6}$	has 1 uterine sibling; no father, grandfather or children
	II	$\frac{1}{3}$	2 or more uterine siblings; no father, grandfather or children
	III	deprived	has a father, grandfather or children

[a] Every relation is in reference to the deceased.

[b] This share is inherited through entitlement (فَرْضِيَة).

[c] This share is inherited through residuaries (عَصَبِيَة).

Table 1.2.a. Females with Stipulated Shares

Inheritor	Case	Share	Condition of deceased
Wife (زوجة)	I	¼	has no children from any marriage
	II	⅛	has children
Daughter (بنت صلبية)	I	½	alone; no son
	II	⅔	2 or more daughters; no son
	III	½ of son's share [a]	has a son
Paternal granddaughter (بنت الابن)	I	½	alone; no son, daughter or grandson
	II	⅔	2 or more granddaughters; no son, daughter or grandson
	III	⅙	has a daughter and no male children
	IV	½ of grandson's share [a]	has a daughter(s) and a grandson has no children and a grandson
	V	deprived	has a son has 2 daughters and no grandsons
Full Sister (أخت عين)	I	½	alone; no full brother, male ascendants or children
	II	⅔	2 or more full sisters; no full brother, male ascendants or children
	III	remainder [b]	has a daughter or granddaughter and no male ascendants or descendants
	IV	½ of brother's share [a]	has a full brother and no male ascendants or male children
	V	deprived	has a father, grandfather, or male children
Consanguine Sister (أخت علات)	I	½	alone; no full siblings or consanguine brother, male ascendants or children
	II	⅔	2 or more consanguine siblings; no full siblings or consanguine brother, male ascendants or children

	III	⅙	has a full sister; no full or consanguine brothers, male ascendants or children
	IV	remainder [b]	only daughter(s) or granddaughter; no full siblings or consanguine brother, male ascendants or children
	V	½ of brother's share [a]	only consanguine brother(s), no full brother, no male ascendants or male children
	VI	deprived	2 full sisters and no consanguine brother, full brother present, one full sister with remainder (if daughter/granddaughter is present
	VII	deprived	has a father, grandfather, or male children

[a] This share is inherited through residuaries through another's right (عَصَبَة بغيره). See next lesson for definitions.

[b] This share is inherited through residuaries along with another's right (عَصَبَة مَعَ الغَيْر). See next lesson for definitions.

Table 1.2.b. Females with Stipulated Shares (continued)

Inheritor	Case	Share	Condition of deceased
Mother (ام)	I	⅓	has no children nor 2 or more siblings of any kind
	II	⅙	has children or 2 or more siblings of any kind
	III	⅓ after spouse's share	only has a spouse and a father
Grandmother (جدة صحيحة)	I	⅙	has one or more grandmothers as long as they are in the same generation
	II	deprived	has a mother, or any closer relation will deprive the further one.

Example 1.1.

Write the stipulated shares of the following heirs.

(a) جدّة ، بنت، أم

(b) زوجة، بنتان، أخ

(c) جد، أم، أب

(a)

ميت

أم	بنت	جدّة
$\frac{1}{6}$	$\frac{1}{2}$	م

(b)

ميت

أخ	بنتان	زوجة
$\frac{1}{6}$	$\frac{2}{3}$	$\frac{1}{8}$

(c)

ميت

أب	أم	جد
ع	$\frac{1}{3}$	م*

*ع: عصبة، م: محجوب

Chapter 2: Residuaries [العَصَبَات]

Residuaries (**'Aṣabāt**) are those heirs with no fixed share in the estate. They inherit the remainder of the estate after the inheritance of the *dhawu al-furūd*, or all of the estate, if there are no *dhawu al-furūḍ* present.

There are two types of 'aṣabāt; 'Aṣaba Nasabī (عَصَبَة نَسَبِي) and 'Aṣaba Sababī (عَصَبَة سَبَبِي).

1. **'Aṣabah Nasabī** are the heirs that are linked to the deceased by way of lineage or family. These will be discussed herein (Figure 2.1).
2. '**Aṣabah Sababī** are the heirs that are linked to the deceased by way of ownership and emancipation, like a master who freed the deceased.

Figure 2.1 Categories of 'Aṣabāt

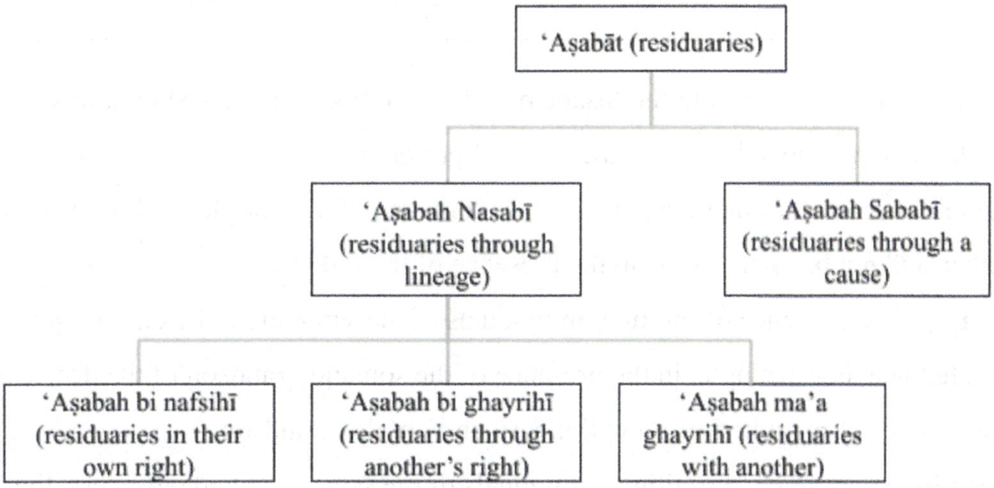

2.1. 'Aṣabah bi Nafsihī (عَصَبَة بِنَفْسِه):

Residuaries in their own right. This refers to the male heir that is linked to the deceased without any female in between. When the term 'aṣabah is used generally, it refers to this subcategory. There are four levels of 'aṣabah bi nafsihī in descending order of preference, as listed in Table 2.1.

Table 2.1. Categories of ʻAṣabah bi Nafsihī

	Category	Description	Inheritors
I	Juz' al-mayyit (جزء الميّت)	progeny of the deceased	male children: son, paternal grandson, etc. downwards
II	Aṣl al-mayyit (أصل الميّت)	ascendant of the deceased	father (أَصْل قَرِيْب), paternal grandfather (أَصْل بَعِيْد), etc. upwards
III	Far' al-aṣl al-qarīb (فرع الأصل القريب)	progeny of the **near** ascendant (i.e., father)	male children of the father: full brother, consanguine brother, full brother's son, consanguine brother's son, etc.
IV	Far' al-aṣl al-ba'īd (فرع الأصل البعيد)	progeny of the **distant** ascendant (i.e., grandfather)	male children of the paternal grandfather: full paternal uncle, consanguine paternal uncle, full uncle's son, consanguine paternal uncle's son

Preference in inheritance is given to the ʻaṣaba bi nafsihī through three considerations:

1. **Rank:** The rank mentioned above is the order of preference. Thus, a person in a lower level will not become ʻaṣaba in the presence of someone of a higher level. For example, the brother will not become ʻaṣaba in the presence of the father. .
2. **Proximity:** In the presence of multiple individuals of the same rank, the closer 'aṣaba' is given preference. For example, in the presence of the son and grandson of the deceased, who are both juz al-mayyit, the son will inherit and not the grandson.
3. **Strength:** In the presence of multiple individuals of the same rank and closeness, the strength of closeness is considered. For example, in the presence of the full brother and the consanguine brother, the full brother will inherit and not the consanguine brother.

2.2. ʻAṣabah bi Ghayrihī (عَصَبَة بِغَيْرِه):

Residuaries in another's rights. The female heir who, in the presence of her brother, will get half of his share. This rule is based on the following verse:

يَسْتَفْتُوْنَكَ ؕ قُلِ اللّٰهُ يُفْتِيْكُمْ فِى الْكَلٰلَةِ ؕ اِنِ امْرُؤٌا هَلَكَ لَيْسَ لَهٗ وَلَدٌ وَّلَهٗۤ اُخْتٌ فَلَهَا نِصْفُ مَا تَرَكَ ۚ وَهُوَ يَرِثُهَاۤ اِنْ لَّمْ يَكُنْ لَّهَا وَلَدٌ ؕ
فَاِنْ كَانَتَا اثْنَتَيْنِ فَلَهُمَا الثُّلُثٰنِ مِمَّا تَرَكَ ؕ وَاِنْ كَانُوْۤا اِخْوَةً رِّجَالًا وَّنِسَآءً **فَلِلذَّكَرِ مِثْلُ حَظِّ الْاُنْثَيَيْنِ** ؕ يُبَيِّنُ اللّٰهُ لَكُمْ اَنْ تَضِلُّوْا ؕ وَاللّٰهُ
بِكُلِّ شَىْءٍ عَلِيْمٌ ۧ (١٧٦)

They ask you ˹for a ruling, O Prophet˺. Say, "Allah gives you a ruling regarding those who die without children or parents." If a man dies childless and leaves behind a sister, she will inherit one-half of his estate, whereas her brother will inherit all of her estate if she dies childless. If this person leaves behind two sisters, they together will inherit two-thirds of the estate. But if the deceased leaves male and female siblings, ***a male's share will be equal to that of two females****. Allah makes ˹this˺ clear to you so you do not go astray. And Allah has ˹perfect˺ knowledge of all things. (176)*

There are two types:

a) Far' al-Mayyit (فَرْعُ الْميّت): Descendents of the deceased (i.e. daughter, granddaughter, great-granddaughter, etc.)

b) Far' aṣl al-Mayyit (فَرْعُ أصْل الْمَيّت): direct descendents of the father of the deceased (i.e. the full sisters and consanguine sisters of the deceased)

Note: the daughters of siblings (i.e., nieces) will not inherit through 'aṣaba bi ghayrihī. They are considered dhawu al-arḥām.

2.3. 'Aṣabah ma'a Ghayrihī (عَصَبَة مَعَ غَيْرِه):

Residuaries with another. This category is restricted to the full or consanguine sisters of the deceased. They are included in the estate as part of the *dhawu al-furūd* together with the daughter or granddaughter of the deceased.

Note: Closeness of the sister is considered in giving preference for inheritance. Thus in the presence of a full sister and a consanguine sister, with the daughter or granddaughter, the full sister will be given preference and the consanguine sister will be deprived.

Example 2.1.

Classify the following heirs with the type and category of 'aṣabah.

(a) paternal grandfather
(b) consanguine sister (in the presence of the brother)
(c) full brother's son

	Type	Category
(a) paternal grandfather	'Aṣabah bi Nafsihī	Aṣl al-mayyit
(b) consanguine sister	'Aṣabah bi Ghayrihī	Far' aṣl al-mayyit
(c) full brother's son	'Aṣabah bi Nafsihī	Far' al-aṣl al-qarīb

Chapter 3: Prevention of an Heir [الحَجَب]

Ḥajab refers to the prevention of certain individuals from inheriting in the presence of a more deserving heir. For example, when the father is present then the grandfather will be prevented. There are 6 individuals who will never be completely deprived from the inheritence. These individuals are the father, mother, husband, wife, son, and daughter. There are 2 types of *ḥajab* (see *Figure 3.1*):

1. **Ḥajab Nuqṣān:** The heir is partially deprived
2. **Ḥajab Ḥirmān:** The heir is totally deprived

A **maḥrūm** (Figure 3.1.) heir cannot reduce or prevent another inheritor. Such an individual has one of the four causes of being prevented from inheritance (refer to Introduction). For example, the disbelieving son will not reduce the share of his mother.

A ***maḥjūb*** heir (Figure 3.1.) can reduce or prevent another inheritor. For example, the sisters will be prevented from inheriting in the presence of the father, however, they will reduce the mother's share from ⅓ to ⅙.

There are 2 ways of recognizing *Ḥajab Ḥirmān:*

1. The closer relative will be given preference, such that the closer relative will deprive the further relative from inheriting. For example, the grandson will be deprived in the presence of the son.
2. If everyone who is connected through the deceased by the means of another individual then in the presence of that individual they will be deprived. For example, the siblings will be deprived in the presence of the father.

   Exception: *Awlād al-umm* (uterine siblings) will not be deprived in the presence of the mother. This is because the mother's share is only ⅓ so there will always be leftover as opposed to the father who inherits through residuaries (عَصَبِيَة).

Figure 3.1. Types of Ḥajab

Ḥajab Nuqṣān (حَجَب نُقْصَان)	**Ḥajab Ḥirmān** (حَجَب حِرْمَان)
The method of **partial** deprivation in the presence of a more deserving heir In such a case, a specific individual's share will be reduced from the stipulated share to a lesser share	The method of **complete** deprivation in the presence of a more deserving heir In such a case, a specific individual will be completely deprived from the inheritance
Examples: husband, wife, mother, paternal granddaughter, and the consanguine sister	**Examples**: grandfather in the presence of the father and the brothers and sisters in the presence of the father

Example 3.1.

Classify the following heirs with the type of *ḥajab*

(a) paternal grandfather in the presence of the father
(b) wife in the presence of children
(c) A son, who is a disbeliever, in the presence of a grandson

	Type
(a) paternal grandfather	*Ḥajab Ḥirmān (*Completely prevented)
(b) wife	*Ḥajab Nuqṣān* (Partially prevented)
(c) son	*Maḥrūm (*will not prevent the grandson)

Chapter 4: Lowest Common Denominator [الْمَخَارِج]

The Lowest Common Denominator (LCD) (***Makhraj***) refers to the lowest common multiple of all the denominators. The LCD is used to calculate the total shares of inheritance. The deceased's estate is divided into shares based on the number and types of heirs.

When adding and subtracting fractions, the denominators of the fractions must be the same. For example, $\frac{1}{4} + \frac{1}{6} = \frac{3}{12} + \frac{2}{12} = \frac{5}{12}$

The denominators 4 and 6 are different. In order to make them the same, a common multiple between them must be found. The multiples of 4 are: 4, 8, 12. The multiples of 6 are: 6, 12, 24. The common multiple is 12. In order to change the denominator of both fractions to 12, the fraction (both the numerator and denominator) are multiplied by the same number. Once the denominators are the same, the numerators can be added or subtracted to solve the equation.

The denominator of the shares can either be:

1. Common (Table 4.1)
2. Different (Table 4.2): Calculate the LCD.

Table 4.1. Common Shares of Dhawu al Furūḍ (in bold) and ʻAṣaba

Stipulated Share	***Makhraj***	**Example** ميـــــــــــــــت	
نصف	2	**أب** $1/2$	**زوج** $1/2$
ربع	4	أخ $3/4$	**زوجة** $1/4$
ثمن	8	**ابن** $7/8$	**زوجة** $1/8$
ثلث	3	أخ $1/3$	**أم** $2/3$
ثلثان	3	عم $2/3$	**بنتان** $1/3$
سدس	6	**ابن** $1/6$	**أم** $5/6$

Table 4.2. Different Shares of Dhawu al Furūḍ (in bold) and ʻAṣaba

Stipulated Share	*Makhraj*	Example ميـــــــــــت		
ثلث وثلثان وسدس	6	**أم** 1/6	**أختان عين** 2/3	أخوان لأم 1/3
نصف وسدس	6	**بنت** 1/2	**جدة** 1/6	ابن الابن 1/3
نصف وثلثان	6	زوج 1/2	**أختان** 2/3	
نصف وثلث	6	**أخت** 1/2	**أم** 1/3	عم 1/6
نصف وثمن	8	**زوجة** 1/8	**بنت** 1/2	أخ 3/8
ربع وثلث	12	**زوجة** 1/4	**أم** 1/3	ابن العم 5/12
ربع وثلثان	12	**زوج** 1/4	**بنتان** 2/3	ابن الأخ 1/12
ربع وسدس	12	**زوج** 1/4	**جدة** 1/6	**ابن** 7/12
ثمن وثلثان	24	**زوجة** 1/8	**بنتان** 2/3	ابن الابن 5/24
ثمن وسدس	24	**زوجة** 1/8	**أم** 1/6	**ابن** 7/24
نصف وثمن وسدس	24	**زوجة** 1/8	**بنت** 1/2	**أم** 1/6 ابن العم 5/24

Example 4.1.

Calculate the *makhraj* of the following group of numbers:

(a) 2, 3	**2** $\times 3 = 6$	Makhraj = 6
(b) 3, 8, 12	**3** $\times 8 = 24$ **12** $\times 2 = 24$	Makhraj= 24
(c) 3, 4, 12	**3** $\times 4 = 12$ **12** $\times 1 = 12$	Makhraj= 12

Chapter 5: Increasing the *Makhraj* [العَول]

If multiple heirs have stipulated shares, and their total is greater the *makhraj*, the *makhraj* may be increased. This is called ***'Awl***. For example, a woman passes away leaving behind her husband (entitled to ½) and 2 sisters (entitled to ⅔). As the LCD is 6, the shares will be rewritten as 3/6 and 4/6. Since that leads to a total of 7/6, the denominator is increased to 7, instead.

The total is increased as follows (Table 5.1):

1. An LCD of 6 can increase to 7, 8, 9 or 10.
2. An LCD of 12 can increase to 13, 15, or 17.
3. An LCD of 24 can only increase to 27.

Table 5.1. Examples of 'Awl

Makhraj	'Awl	**Example** ميـــــــــــت	**Solution**
6	7	زوج ½ ، أختان عين ⅔	LCD = 6 Shares = 7
6	8	زوج ½ ، أختان ⅔ ، أم ⅙	LCD = 6 Shares = 8
6	9	زوج ½ ، أختان عين ⅔ ، أختان لأم ⅓	LCD = 6 Shares = 9
6	10	زوج ½ ، أختان عين ⅔ ، أختان لأم ⅓ ، جدة ⅙	LCD = 6 Shares = 10
12	13	زوجة ¼ ، أختان عين ⅔ ، أم ⅙	LCD = 12 Shares = 13
12	15	زوجة ¼ ، أختان عين ⅔ ، أختان لأم ⅓	LCD = 12 Shares = 15
12	17	زوجة ¼ ، أختان عين ⅔ ، أختان لأم ⅓ ، أم ⅙	LCD = 12 Shares = 17
24	27	زوجة ⅛ ، بنتان ⅔ ، أم ⅙ ، أب ⅙	LCD = 24 Shares = 27

Example 5.1.

Calculate the ʻAwl in each group of heirs.

(a) أم، زوجة، أختان

(b) زوج، (٤) أخوات

(c) زوج، (٣) جدّات، (٦) أخوات

ميـــــــــــــــــــــــــــت	Makhraj	ʻAwl
أم ⅙ ، زوجة ¼ ، أختان ⅔	12	13
زوج ½ ، (٤) أخوات ⅔	6	7
زوج ½ ، (٣) جدّات ⅙ ، (٦) أخوات ⅔	6	8

Chapter 6: Relationship between Numbers

There are four types of relationships between two numbers (Figure 6.1.). They are:

1. ***Tamāthul* (تَمَاثُل)**: Two numbers are the same (i.e. 2 and 2)
2. ***Tadākhul* (تَدَاخُل)**: The smaller number is a factor of the larger number (i.e. 2 and 8)
3. ***Tawāfuq* (تَوَافُق)**: The smaller number is not a factor of the larger number, but both share a separate common factor besides 1 (i.e. 6 and 9 both have a common factor of 3)
4. ***Tabāyun* (تَبَايُن)**: Two numbers have only 1 as a common factor, also called prime factors.

Figure 6.1. Visual representation of number relations

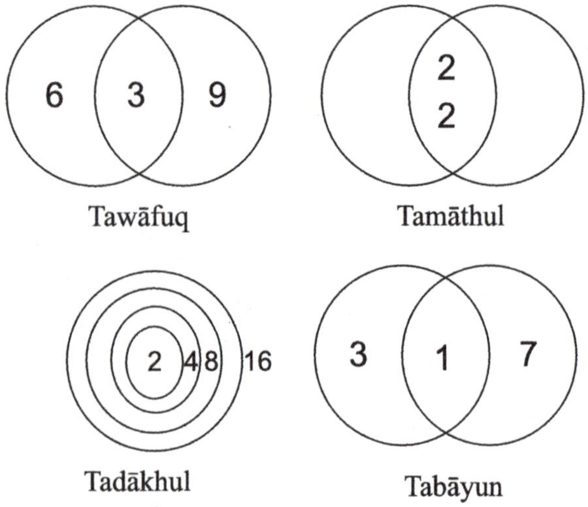

Example 6.1.

Identify the relationship between the following pairs of numbers:

(a) 6, 9: <u>*Tawāfuq*</u> Reason: both have a common factor of 3.

(b) 8, 16: <u>*Tadākhul*</u> Reason: both have common factors of 8, 4, 2 and 1.

(c) 3, 7: <u>*Tabāyun*</u> Reason: no common factor

Chapter 7: Rectification of Inherited Shares

[التَّصْحِيح]

Taṣḥīḥ means to rectify and it refers to the process of avoiding decimals. In a case where there are multiple individuals (***ru'ūs***) in one group of inheritors, such as more than one sister, and the shares (***sihām***) allocated to them cannot be divided amongst them without using decimals, then we will apply one of the following rules of taṣḥīḥ. This fraction (***kasr***) in a group is thus avoided by the process of taṣḥīḥ.

To assess the relationship between sihām and ru'ūs, there are 7 rules of taṣḥīḥ:

(a) The following rules are applied to differences within only 1 group (***farīq***) of heirs. In such a case, we will look at the relationship between the sihām and ru'ūs.

***Rule #0. Tamāthul*:** If the *ru'ūs* and the *sihām* are the same, then leave the question as is.
Rule #1. Tadākhul: Take the *ru'ūs* as the multiplication factor (*madhrūb*).
***Rule #2. Tawāfuq*:** Simplify the fraction and take the quotient (*wifq*) of the *ru'ūs* as the *madhrūb*.
***Rule #3. Tabāyun*:** Take the *ru'ūs* as the *madhrūb*.

(b) The following rules are applied to differences amidst 2 or more groups of heirs. In such a case, we will look at the relationship between the different ru'ūs.

***Rule #4. Tamāthul* between two or more *farīq*:** Take the number of heirs in any group as the *madhrūb*.

***Rule #5. Tadākhul* between two or more *farīq*:** Take the larger number of ru'ūs as *madhrūb*.
***Rule #6. Tawāfuq* between two or more *farīq*:** Take the *wifq* of one group multiplied by the heirs of the other group to get the *madhrūb*.

***Rule # 7. Tabāyun* between two or more *farīq*:** Multiply both numbers to get the *madhrūb*.

Comparing more than two numbers in a different order will yield the same result, although the sequence of relations identified may differ.

Example 7.1.

Calculate the *madhrūb* in each group of numbers. Identify the *wifq* (quotient).

(a) 4, 9, 6

(i) 4 and 9: Tabāyun Apply Rule #7, multiply both numbers → 36

(ii) 36 and 6: _Tadākhul_ Apply Rule #5, take the large number → 36, *wifq* is 6 and 1 respectively.

(b) 6, 9, 4

(i) 6 and 9: _Tawāfuq_ Apply Rule #6 → 18, *wifq* is 2 and 3 respectively.

(ii) 18 and 4: _Tawāfuq_ Apply Rule #6 → 36, *wifq* is 9 and 2 respectively.

The rules of *taṣḥīḥ* within only 1 group of heirs are:

1. *Tadākhul*: take the *ru'ūs* as the multiplication factor (*madhrūb*).

Example 7.2.

Identify the group with kasr. Calculate all shares.

(a) زوجة، (٦) أعمام

	/24
مضروب: 6	/4
ت	ميـ
(٦) أعمام	زوجة
ع	¼
3	1
18	6

2. *Tawāfuq*: simplify the fraction and take the quotient (*wifq*) of the *ru'ūs* as the *madhrūb*.

Example 7.3.

Identify the group with kasr. Calculate all shares.

(a) أم، أب،(٦) بنات

		/18
مضروب: 3		/6
ت		ميـ
(٦) بنات	أب	أم
⅔	⅙ + ع	⅙
4	0 + 1	1
12	3	3

3. *Tabāyun*: take the *ru'ūs* as the *madhrūb.*

Example 7.4.

Identify the group with kasr. Calculate all shares.

(a) (٤) زوجات، أم، بنت، عم

			/96
مضروب: 4			/24
ت			مي
عم	بنت	أم	(٤) زوجات
ع	$\frac{1}{2}$	$\frac{1}{6}$	$\frac{1}{8}$
5	12	4	3
20	48	16	12

The rules of *taṣḥīḥ* multiple groups of heirs are:

4. *Tamāthul* between two *farīq*: take the number of heirs in a group as the *madhrūb.*

Example 7.5.

Identify the groups with kasr. Calculate all shares.

(a) زوجتان، ابنان، أم

		/48
مضروب: 2		/24
ت		مي
أم	ابنان	زوجتان
$\frac{1}{6}$	ع	$\frac{1}{8}$
4	17	3
8	34	6

5. *Tadākhul* between two *farīq*: take the larger number as *madhrūb*.

Example 7.6.

Identify the groups with kasr. Calculate all shares.

(a) (٤) زوجات، جدّتان، (١٢) اعمام

		/144
مضروب: 12		/12
ت		ميـ
(١٢) اعمام	جدّتان	(٤) زوجات
ع	1/6	1/4
7	2	3
84	24	36

6. *Tawāfuq* between two *farīq*: take the *wifq* of one group multiplied by the heirs of the other group to get the *madhrūb*.

Example 7.7.

Identify the groups with kasr. Calculate all shares.

(a) زوج، (٣) جدّات، (٦) أخوات

		/144
مضروب: 18		/6 → /8
ت		ميـ
(٩) أخوات	(٦) جدّات	زوج
2/3	1/6	1/2
4	1	3
72	18	54

7. *Tabāyun* between two *farīq*: multiply both numbers to get the *madhrūb*.

Example 7.8.

Identify the groups with kasr. Calculate all shares.

a) زوجة، (٣) أخوات، (٤) جدّات، (٥) اعمام

			/720
مضروب: 60			/12
(٥) اعمام	(٤) جدّات	(٣) أخوات	زوجة

ميت

(٥) اعمام	(٤) جدّات	(٣) أخوات	زوجة
ع	1/6	1/2	1/4
1	2	6	3
60	120	360	180

PART 2: DISTRIBUTION

Chapter 8: Distribution of Estate

If the total value of the estate (***tarikah***) is known, after completing the *taṣḥīḥ*, divide the estate amongst the heirs based on their shares. The following method will be applied in dividing the estate:

1. Use the relationships between the estate and *taṣḥīḥ* to calculate the individual shares.
   a. If there is *tawāfuq* between the estate and *taṣḥīḥ*, multiply each share by the *wifq* of the estate.
   b. If there is *tabāyun* between the estate and *taṣḥīḥ*, multiply each share by the estate. Then, divide the *taṣḥīḥ* with the quotient.
2. Multiply the shares with the total value of the estate to get the amount owed to each heir.
3. If there are decimal fractions, multiply the denominator with the *taṣḥīḥ* and take the quotient as the new *taṣḥīḥ*.
4. Add all of the individual shares to check the total.

Formula: (siham x tarikah)/makhraj

Example 8.1.

A man passed away leaving behind his father, mother, wife and two daughters. His estate is worth $80. Calculate the amount each heir inherits.

/27

تركة: 80 　　　　/24 → /27

ت ——— ميـ

بنت	بنت	زوجة	أم	أب
⅔		⅛	⅙	⅙ + ع
16		3	4	4
$\frac{8\times80}{27}$	$\frac{8\times80}{27}$	$\frac{3\times80}{27}$	$\frac{4\times80}{27}$	$\frac{4\times80}{27}$
$ 23.70	$ 23.70	$ 8.89	$ 11.85	$ 11.85

$ 79.99, remaining $ 0.01 is given to charity.

Example 8.2.

Distribute an estate of $7.25 amongst a husband, mother, two full sisters and one full brother.

مضروب: 4	/48
تركة: 7.25	/12

ميـــت

أخت	أخت	أخ	أم	زوج
	ع		⅙	½
	4		2	6
$\frac{1\times29}{48}$	$\frac{1\times29}{48}$	$\frac{2\times29}{48}$	$\frac{2\times29}{48}$	$\frac{6\times29}{48}$
$ 0.60	$ 0.60	$ 1.21	$ 1.21	$ 3.63

$ 7.25

Chapter 9: Distribution amongst Creditors

Creditors, or those giving loans, are to be paid from the deceased's estate (***tarikah***). If the debts (***dayn***) are more than the estate, the estate is divided accordingly.

1. Write the debt owed to each creditor like a share. Make the entire debt the *taṣḥīḥ*.
2. Consider the relationship between the *tarikah* and *dayn*. Simplify the ratio.
4. Multiply each individual debt by the ratio to get individual shares.

Example 9.1.

Fatimah passed away owing Abdullah $10, Ramlah $20, Sidrah $50 and Zubayr $20. She left behind $10. Calculate how much each lender will receive.

تركة: 10/ | دين: 100/

ميــــــــــــــــــــــــــــــت

زبير	سدرة	رملة	عبد الله
20	50	20	10
$\frac{20\times10}{100}$	$\frac{50\times10}{100}$	$\frac{20\times10}{100}$	$\frac{10\times10}{100}$
$ 2	$ 5	$ 2	$ 1

Example 9.2.

Karim passed away leaving $6.50. He owes Sharif $2, Husayn $3, Ilyas $4 and Najib $5. Calculate the amount each creditor will receive from the deceased's estate.

مضروب: 2 | /28

تركة: 6.50 | دين: 14/

ميــــــــــــــــــــــــــــــت

نجيب	إلياس	حسين	شريف
5	4	3	2
$\frac{5\times13}{28}$	$\frac{4\times13}{28}$	$\frac{3\times13}{28}$	$\frac{2\times13}{28}$
$ 2.32	$ 1.86	$ 1.39	$ 0.93

Chapter 10: Settlement [التَّخَارُج]

In the case that one or more of the inheritors reach a settlement and agree to forfeit their inheritance share, they are removed from the inheritance. This process is called ***Takhāruj***.

1. Identify the heirs who have agreed to a settlement. Write the reason for settlement.
2. Solve the question as usual.
3. Subtract the shares that have been settled for from the *taṣḥīḥ*.
4. Make the calculation from the leftover shares.

Example 10.1.

Maria is survived by her husband, mother and father. The husband settles to give up his share in inheritance for the dowry owed to Maria.

		/3	
		/6	
ميـــت			
أب	أم	زوج	*Settlement*
ع	$\frac{1}{3}$ after زوج	$\frac{1}{2}$	صالح على مهر
2	1	3	-3
2	1		

Chapter 11: Redistribution [الرَّدّ]

After the initial distribution of the estate to the *Dawu al-furūḍ*, if there are no *'Aṣabāt* present, it will be redistributed to the *Dawul furūḍ* a second time. *Radd* only takes place on the *Dawu al-furūḍ al-nasabī* called the ***Man yuraddu 'alayhim***. The inheritance is not to be redistributed to the *Dawu al-furūḍ al-sababī* (i.e., spouses) called the ***Man lā yuradd 'alayhim*** *(Table 10.1)*.

Table 11.1. Summary of Radd Rules

Rule #		*Man yuraddu 'alayhim*	*Man lā yuraddu 'alayhim*
1	Make the *makhraj* the *ru'ūs*	One type	None
2	Make the *makhraj* the *sihām*	Multiple types	None
3	Make the makhraj from the total share of the spouse (*Man lā yuradd)*	One type	Spouse
4	Apply Rule #3 then Rule #2	Multiple types	Spouse

Rule #1: If there is only one type of *Man yuradd*, make the *makhraj* the *ru'ūs*.

Example 11.1.

A man passes away, leaving behind only 6 daughters. How much will they inherit?

مي———————————ت

بنت	بنت	بنت	بنت	بنت	بنت	**تصحيح/**
		$\frac{2}{3}$				/3
		Apply Rule 1				ردّ
1	1	1	1	1	1	**/6**

Rule #2: If there are multiple types of *Man yuradd*, make the *makhraj* the *sihām*.

Example 11.2.

A man leaves behind a uterine brother, uterine sister and mother. How much do they inherit?

ميـــــــــــــــــــــــــــــــــــت

أخت لأم	أخ لأم	أم	تصحيح/
	$\frac{1}{3}$	$\frac{1}{6}$	/6
	2	1	/3
	Apply Rule 2		ردّ
1	1	1	**/3**

Rule #3: If there are both categories with one type of *Man yuradd,* make the *makhraj* the total share of the spouse (*Man lā yuradd)*. Give the spouse the minimum amount.

Example 11.3.

A woman leaves behind her husband and 3 daughters. How much will they inherit?

ميـــت

بنت	بنت	بنت	زوج	تصحيح/
	$\frac{2}{3}$		$\frac{1}{4}$	/12
	8		3	/11
	Apply Rule 3			ردّ
1	1	1	1	**/4**

Rule #4: If there are both categories with multiple types of *Man yuradd*, apply Rule 3 and then Rule 2.

a. Compare new *taṣḥīḥ* (from Rule 2) with previous *taṣḥīḥ* (from Rule 3).
b. If the relationship is of *tawāfuq* or *tabāyun*, multiply both *taṣḥīḥ* together to get the final *taṣḥīḥ*.
c. Multiply the *Man yuradd* with the *mā fī al-yad.*
d. Multiply the *Man lā yuradd* with the new *taṣḥīḥ*.

Example 11.4.

A man leaves behind his two wives, mother, grandmother and 4 daughters. How much will they inherit?

ميـــت

مضروب	بنت	بنت	بنت	بنت	جدّة	أم	زوجة	زوجة	**تصحيح/**
			$\frac{2}{3}$		م	$\frac{1}{6}$	$\frac{1}{8}$		/24
			16		0	4	3		/23
				Apply Rule 3					ردّ
ما في اليد				ما في اليد - 7			1		/8
				Apply Rule 2					
			4			1			/5
				Compare new and old taṣḥīḥ					
× 7			(28			7)	5		/40
× 2			56			14	10		**/80**

Chapter 12: Inheritance in Multiple Generations [المُنَاسَخَة]

Munāsakhah is the distribution of the estate of a deceased heir. This occurs in a case where a person passes away and their estate is not distributed immediately. After some time, when the estate is distributed, some of the heirs from the original distribution have passed away. Thus, the shares of the heirs are passed on to the next generation of inheritors.

The steps to solve the case are:

1. Title the response *huwa al-muwāfiq* which means "Allāh is the One who gives ability".
2. Identify the person who passed away first (***mūrith a'lā***). Indicate the deceased by circling his shares in the case. Calculate the distribution of his heirs, individually.
3. For each subsequent generation, add the shares that one received from the previous generation (***mā fī al-yad***).
4. Compare the *makhraj* of the current case with the *mā fī al-yad* or shares inherited from the previous generation. If there is *tawāfuq* between these two numbers, reduce them to the lowest form.
5. Multiply the *makhraj* of this case with all heirs alive above and the *mā fī al-yad* with all heirs of the current case.
6. Calculate the final shares of all living heirs (***mablagh***) by adding the shares from each case.
7. Calculate the percentage share from the total estate worth.

Example 13.1

Yusuf passed away in 1939 leaving behind: 2 wives (Fatimah, Aishah), 3 full sisters (Maariyah, Zahidah, Maryam), 2 grandmothers (Khadijah, Humayrah), 3 daughters (Asma, Maymunah, Rayhanah) and 2 sons (Ismail, Mustafah).

In 1956, Mustafah, the son of Yusuf passed away leaving behind: mother (Fatimah), 3 sisters (Asma, Maymunah, Rayhanah), brother (Ismail) and wife (Zainab).

In 1975, Maymunah passed away leaving behind 2 sons (Khalil and Khalid) and a daughter (Zahrah). The property is worth $500,200. Calculate the share of each inheritor.

	/30 240
/14	/5040
/15	/336
مضروب: 6/	/24

يوسف (م١٩٣٩) ميت

اخوات (٣)	بنت ميمونة	بنت ريحانة	بنت أسماء	ابن إسماعيل	ابن مصطفى	جدّة خديجة	جدّة حميرة	زوجة عائشة	زوجة فاطمة
م			ع			⅙		⅛	
0	34	34	34	68	68	28	28	21	21
0	510	510	510	1020	-	420	420	315	315
0	-	3060	3060	6120	-	2520	2520	1890	1890

The relationship between *mā fī al-yad* (68) and *makhraj* (60) is *tawāfuq* (common factor = 4). Hence, all shares above are multiplied by 15 and all shares below are multiplied by 17.

/6	
/17	
مضروب: 5/	/60

مصطفى (م١٩٥٦) ميت

أخ إسماعيل	أخت ميمونة	أخت ريحانة	أخت أسماء	زوجة زينب	أم فاطمة
	ع			¼	⅙
	7			3	2
14	7	7	7	15	10
238	119	119	119	255	170
1428	-	714	714	1530	1020

The relationship between *mā fī al-yad* (119 + 510 = 629) and *makhraj* (6) is *tabāyun*. Hence, all shares above are multiplied by 6 and all shares below are multiplied by 629.

/6	مضروب: 629/

ميمونة (١٩٧٥م) ميـــــــــــــــــــــــــــت

أم فاطمة	ابن خليل	ابن خالد	بنت زهرة
1/6		ع	
1	2	2	1
629	1258	1258	629

The shares of each inheritor are:

Inheritor	**Shares (of 30 240)**	**Estate Worth (of $500 200)**
Ismail	6120 + 1428 = 7548	124 851.51
Asma	3060 + 714 = 3774	62 425.75
Rayhana	3060 + 714 = 3774	62 425.75
Khadija	2520	41 683.33
Humayra	2520	41 683.33
Aisha	1890	31 262.50
Fatima	1890 + 1020 + 629 = 3539	58 538.62
Zaynab	1530	25 307.74
Zahra	629	10 404.29
Khalid	1258	20 808.59
Khalil	1258	20 808.59
Total		**500 199.999**

Chapter 13: Maternal Relations [ذَوُو الأَرْحَام]

Maternal relatives who are not *dhawu al-furūḍ* or *ʿaṣabāt.*

Table 6.1. Categories of Dhawu al-arḥām

	Category	Description	Inheritors
I	Juz' al-mayyit (جزء الميّت)	progeny linked through a female	daughter's children, paternal granddaughter's children
II	Aṣl al-mayyit (أصل الميّت)	ascendant linked through a female	*fāsid* grandfather (i.e., mother between him and *mayyit*) and grandmother (i.e., *jaddah fāsidah* between her and *mayyit*)
III	Far' al-aṣl al-qarīb (فرع الأصل القريب)	progeny of the **near** ascendant (i.e., father)	male/female children of full (عين) sister or female descendents of full (عين), consanguine (علّات) or uterine (أخياف) brother
IV	Far' al-aṣl al-ba'īd (فرع الأصل البعيد)	progeny of the **distant** ascendant (i.e., grandfather)	paternal aunt, uterine uncle, maternal uncle or aunt and their children, female descendents of uterine (أخياف) uncle and daughters of full (عين) uncle

Category I: Progeny linked through a female

In the absence of the *dhawu al-furūḍ* and the *ʿaṣabāt* , the *dhawu al-arḥām* will inherit the entire estate.

The inheritance will be distributed as such:

0. If all types of *dhawu al-arḥām* are present, only the first type will inherit.

Example 14.1

Write the shares of a maternal grandfather, niece and maternal uncle.

ميـــــــــــــــــــــــــــــــــــــــت

جدّ فاسد	بنت العم	عمة
1	م	م

1. In the presence of heirs from the same categories, only those closest to the deceased (*al-aqrab min al-mayyit*) will inherit.

Example 14.2

Write the shares of a paternal great-granddaughter and paternal great-great-granddaughter.

ميـــــــــــــــــــــــــت

I	بنت	بنت
II	بنت	بنت
III	بنت	ابن
IV	ابن	
	م	1

2. In the presence of multiple heirs from Category I (*far'u mayyit*), the child of the heir (*walad al-wārith*) will inherit **not** the children of *dhawu al-arḥām*.

Example 14.3

Write the shares of a paternal great-granddaughter and maternal great-grandson.

ميـــــــــــــــــــــــــت

I	بنت	ابن
II	بنت	بنت
III	ابن	بنت
	م	1

3. If all are either w*alad al-wārith* or *walad dhawil arḥām*, then all males and females inherit equally.

Example 14.4

Write the shares of two granddaughters.

ميـــــــــــــــــــــــــت

I	بنت	بنت
II	بنت	بنت
	1	1

4. If there are different *dhawu al-arḥām* in terms of male and female, then males will inherit twice the share of females. However, in principle they are the same, i.e., with the same ascendent.

Example 14.5

Write the shares of a grandson and a granddaughter.

ميـــــــــــــــــــــــت

I	بنت	بنت
II	ابن	بنت
	2	1

5. If the parents of the *dhawu al-arḥām* differ in terms of male and female in one generation, then the males will inherit twice the share of females and that will be given to the children.

Example 14.6

Calculate the shares of the following heirs over multiple generations.

ميـــــــــــــــــــــــت

I	بنت	بنت
II	بنت	ابن
III	ابن	بنت
	1	2

6. If there are differences in terms of male and female in multiple generations, then separate groups of male and female. Then divide the parents' share equally among the children if they are the same gender otherwise the males will inherit twice the share of females.

Example 14.7

Calculate the shares of the following heirs over multiple generations.

/60

مضروب: 4/ — /15

ميت

I	ابن	ابن	ابن	بنت	بنت	بنت	بنت	بنت	بنت	بنت	بنت	بنت
		6						9				
		24						36				
II	بنت	بنت	بنت	بنت	بنت	بنت	بنت	بنت	بنت	بنت	بنت	بنت
III	ابن	بنت	بنت	بنت	بنت	بنت	بنت	بنت	بنت	ابن	ابن	ابن
	12	12					18				18	
IV	بنت	بنت	بنت	بنت	بنت	بنت	ابن	ابن	ابن	بنت	بنت	ابن
	12	12			6			12		9		9
V	بنت	ابن	بنت	ابن	بنت	بنت	بنت	بنت	ابن	بنت	بنت	بنت
	12	8	4	3	3			6	6	9		9
VI	بنت	بنت	بنت	بنت	ابن	بنت	ابن	بنت	بنت	ابن	بنت	بنت
	12	8	4	3	2	1	4	2	6	6	3	9

7. If there are a number of children from parents, their progeny is considered.

Example 14.8

Calculate the shares of the following heirs over multiple generations.

			/28
	/4		/7
	ت		مي
I	ابن	بنت	بنت
	4	3	
	16	12	
II	بنت	ابن	بنت (۲)
	16	6	6
III	بنتين	بنت	ابنين
	8-8	6	3-3

8. Consider the multiple links of the deceased.

Example 14.9

Calculate the shares of the heirs of married cousins.

			/28
	/4		/7
	ت		مي
I	بنت	بنت	بنت
	1	1	1
II	بنت	بنت (۲)	ابن (۲)
	1	2	4
III	ابن	بنتين	
	6	6-16	
	6	3-3-8-8	
	6	11-11	

Category II: Ascendent linked through a female

The inheritance will be distributed as such:

1. If there are relatives close/ further from the deceased, the closer inheritors will inherit.

Example 14.10

Calculate the shares of the maternal grandfather and the mother's maternal grandfather.

ميـــــــــــــــت

I	أم	أم
II	أب	أم
III	-	أب
	1	م

2. If all are equal in closeness, see if the maternal and paternal sides are equal or different. If they are different, then the inheritance ratio will be 2:1.

Example 14.11

Calculate the shares of the paternal great-grandfather and maternal great-grandfather.

ميـــــــــــــــت

I	أب	أم
II	أم	أم
III	أب	أب
	2	1

3. If they are equal in relation (i.e., both the maternal and paternal sides), then see if there is a difference in generation in being male or female. If so, the males will inherit twice the share of females.

Example 14.12

Calculate the shares of the maternal great-grandfather and maternal great-grandmother.

ميـــــــــــــــت

I	أم	أم
II	أب	أب
III	أب	أم
	2	1

Category III: Progeny of deceased's parents

1. The closest to the deceased will inherit.

Example 14.13

Calculate the shares of the sister's grandson and the brother's granddaughter.

	ميت	
I	أخت	أخ
II	بنت	ابن
III	ابن	بنت
	م	1

2. If they are all equal, then the child of the heir (وَلَدُ الوَارِث) is given preference over the *dhawu al-arḥām* child.

Example 14.14

Calculate the shares of the brother's granddaughter and the sister's grandson.

	ميت	
I	أخ	أخت
II	ابن	بنت
III	بنت	ابن
	1	م

3. The strength of closeness is preferred.

Example 14.15

Calculate the shares of the grandchildren of the full, uterine and consanguine brothers.

		ميت	
I	أخ أخياف	أخ علات	أخ عين
II	ابن	بنت	ابن
III	بنت	ابن	بنت
	م	م	1

4. In case of relatives with one rank (e.g., uterine children), an equal share is given. The difference in lineage is not taken into consideration.

Example 14.16

Calculate the shares of the uterine brother's son and the uterine sister's daughter.

ميـــــــــــــــــــــت

I	أخ أخياف	أخت أخياف
II	ابن	بنت
	1	1

5. If all the real children are of one level or all are consanguineous and equal in terms of male and female, the inheritance will be equally distributed.

Example 14.17

Calculate the shares of the full sister's granddaughters.

ميـــــــــــــــــــــت

I	أخت عين	أخت عين
II	بنت	بنت
	1	1

6. If the full children are all equal on one level or consanguine children are equal in terms of male and female and the children are different, then the estate is divided 2:1.

Example 14.18

Calculate the shares of the grandson and granddaughter of the consanguine sister.

ميـــــــــــــــــــــت

I	أخت علات	أخت علات
II	ابن	بنت
	2	1

7. If the parents differ in terms of male and female, the estate will be distributed from the first generation where there is a difference. The parent's share will be given to the child.

Example 14.19

Calculate the shares of the brother's daughter and the full/consanguine sister's son.

ميـــــت

I	أخ	أخت
II	بنت	ابن
	2	1

8. If the *dhawu al-arḥām* differ from the real children, consanguine children and uterine children, or from two groups, then according to the view of Imam Muhammad (raḥimahu Allāh), the estate will be divided amongst the parents first.

Example 14.20

Calculate the shares of the following heirs over multiple generations.

ميـــــت

I	أخ عين	أخت عين	أخ أخياف	أخت أخياف	أخ علات	أخت علات
II	بنت	ابن-بنت	بنت	ابن-بنت	بنت	ابن-بنت
	4	1-2	1	1-1	م	م

Category IV: Progeny of the deceased's paternal grandfather or grandmother

There are two types of progeny of the deceased's grandparents, either without an intermediate link like the maternal aunt or with an intermediate like the children of the maternal aunt.

Type 1

1. If one is alone, he/she will inherit the entire wealth. For example, the paternal aunt.
2. If they are equal in being maternal/paternal (جِهَةُ القَرَابَة), then the strongest relation is given preference. For example, the full paternal aunt is given preference over the consanguine paternal aunt.
3. If they are equal in terms of males and female, whether maternal/paternal and having the same strength of relationship (قُوَّةُ القَرَابَة), then the estate is divided equally. For example, two full aunts will receive equal shares.
4. If they differ in terms of males and females, then the estate is divided 2:1. For example, the uterine uncle will get twice as much as the uterine aunt.
5. If they differ in both the direction (i.e., maternal/paternal) and gender (i.e., males/females), then the paternal side will inherit ⅔ while the maternal side gets ⅓. In this case, the strength of a relationship is irrelevant. For example, the consanguine, paternal aunt will get two-thirds while the full, maternal aunt gets one-third.

Type 2

1. The closest relation inherits. For example, the maternal aunt's son will deprive the maternal aunt's grandson.
2. The strength of the relationship (قُوَّةُ القَرَابَة) is considered. The rank (دَرَجَة) and direction (جِهَة) of the relationship are the same. For example, the full aunt's daughter will deprive the uterine uncle's son.
3. In the case that everything is equal, the child of the *ʿaṣabāh* will be preferred over that of the *dhawu al-arḥām*. For example, the full uncle's daughter will deprive the full aunt's son.
4. The strength of the relation is considered whether the children are of the *ʿaṣabāh* or not. For example, the granddaughter of the full aunt will deprive the granddaughter of the consanguine uncle.
5. If they are equal in closeness (دَرَجَة) but differ in being maternal/paternal (جِهَةُ القَرَابَة) then ⅔ is given to the paternal relation and ⅓ to the maternal relation. For example, the daughter of the full, paternal aunt will be given ⅔ while the son of the full, maternal aunt will be given ⅓.

6. If there are no children, the estate goes to the uncles, aunts, maternal uncles and aunts of the parents and their children. Then, it goes to the uncles and aunts (maternal and paternal) of the grandparents and their children.

Example 14.21

Calculate the shares of the following heirs over multiple generations.

ميت

I	عمّة علات	عمّة علات	عم علات	خالة علات	خالة علات	خال علات
II	بنت	ابن	بنت	بنت	ابن	بنت
III	ابنين	بنتين		بنتين	ابنين	
	4	10	10	2	5	5

PART 3: OTHER APPLICATIONS

Chapter 14: Distribution of the Grandfather [مُقَاسَمَةُ الْجَدّ]

The distribution of the estate in the presence of a grandfather ***(Jadd Ṣaḥīḥ)***.

There are two opinions:

1. Abū Bakr: All siblings will be deprived in the presence the grandfather, similar to when the father is present. This is the view of Imam Abu Hanifah and the *muftā bihi.*
2. Zayd bin Thābit: The real siblings and consanguine siblings will inherit in the presence of grandfather. According to him, the grandfather will be considered a brother and this distribution is known as ***Muqāsamah***.

When there are other individuals from *dawul furūḍ,* then the grandfather will be given the best of three cases:

1. *Muqāsamah*
2. One-third of the remainder of the estate
3. One-sixth of the entire wealth

When there are no individuals from *dawul furūḍ*, then the grandfather will receive the best of the two following cases:

1. *Muqāsamah*
2. One-third of the entire estate

Example 12.1

The deceased leaves a brother, grandfather and husband. What is the best case scenario for the grandfather?

(a) *Muqāsamah*

/2

مضروب: 2/   /4

ميـــت

زوج	جدّ	أخ
½	½	

	1	1
1	1	2

(b) One-third of the remainder of the estate

/6

مضروب: 3 /2

ميـــــــــــــــــــــــــــــــــــــــراث

أخ	جدّ	زوج
ع	⅓ of ع	½
	1	1
⅔	⅓	1
2	1	3

(c) One-sixth of the entire wealth

/6

ميـــــــــــــــــــــــــــــــــــــــراث

أخ	جدّ	زوج
ع	⅙	½
2	1	3

Compare the grandfather's share in each of the three cases:

Muqāsamah	⅓ of remainder	⅙ of all
¼	⅙	⅙

The best case scenario is *Muqāsamah*, hence, the grandfather will receive ¼ of the estate.

Example 12.2

The deceased leaves a brother, grandfather and husband. What is the best case scenario for the grandfather?

(a) *Muqāsamah*

/2

ميت

أخ		جدّ
	ع	
1		1

(b) One-third of the entire estate.

/3

مضروب: 3 /1

ميت

أخ	جدّ
ع	$\frac{1}{3}$
$\frac{2}{3}$	$\frac{1}{3}$
2	1

Compare the grandfather's share in each of the two cases:

Muqāsamah	$\frac{1}{3}$ of all
$\frac{1}{2}$	$\frac{1}{3}$

The best case scenario is *Muqāsamah*, hence, the grandfather will receive $\frac{1}{2}$ of the estate.

Chapter 15: Unborn Child [الحَمْل]

The distribution of unborn heirs is based on the assumed gender and number of heirs. The unborn child (***ḥaml***) is assumed to be a male or female, based on the assumption of who will get more. The present heirs are given the lesser amount and the suspended amount is returned to them after the gender is confirmed at birth, if applicable.

1. Solve the case twice, first assuming the unborn child is a single female and then a single male.
2. Identify in which case, the unborn child will get **more** by comparing the two *taṣḥīḥ* calculations:
   a. If there is *tawāfuq* between them, multiply the *wifq* of one by the total of the other.
   b. If there is *tabāyun* between them, multiply the total of one by the total of the other.
3. Cross multiply the shares of one case with the total or the *wifq* of the *taṣḥiḥ* of the other.
4. Give each of the present heirs the lesser of the two conditions ((أَسْوَأ الحَالَيْن), either *hirmān* or *nuqṣān*. Suspend the better condition until the gender is confirmed at birth.
5. After birth, if the lesser condition is proven, then leave it. Otherwise, return the suspended amount to the heirs.

Example 15.1.

A man passed away, leaving behind an estate worth $500 000. He is survived by his pregnant wife, mother, father, two daughters and a brother. Calculate the shares which must be given to the heirs immediately.

Assuming female

						/2592
/32						/81
مضروب: 3/						/24 → / 27

ميـــــــــــــــــــــــــــــــــت

حمل (أنثى)	بنت	بنت	أخ	أب	أم	زوجة
	⅔		م	⅙	⅙	⅛
	16		0	4	4	3
16	16	16	0	12	12	9
512	512	512	0	<u>384</u>*	<u>384</u>	<u>288</u>

Assuming male

						/2592
/27						/96
مضروب: 4/						/24

ميـــــــــــــــــــــــــــــــــت

حمل (ذكر)	بنت	بنت	أخ	أب	أم	زوجة
	ع		م	⅙	⅙	⅛
	13		0	4	4	3
26	13	13	0	16	16	12
702	*<u>351</u>	<u>351</u>	0	432	432	324

* The underlined shares are distributed immediately.

Chapter 16: Hermaphrodite [الْخُنْثَى]

The hermaphrodite (***khunthā***) is the person with both male and female genitalia. Whichever of the two parts is dominant, it will take its ruling. If both parts are equal, it will be a *khunthā mushkilah.*

The worst of two conditions is given, assuming it's a male or female.

1. Solve the case twice, first assuming the *khunthā* is a male and then a female.
2. Distribute the shares based on which case the *khunthā* will get **less** (أَسْوَأُ الحَلَيْن)**.** This is similar to the case of the Unborn Child (Lesson 15).

Example 16.1.

A woman passed away leaving behind 5 children. She has 3 sons, a daughter and a hermaphrodite. Calculate the shares which must be given to the heirs immediately.

Assuming female.

/8

ميت

خنثى (بنت)	بنت	ابن	ابن	ابن
		ع		
1*	1	2	2	2

Assuming male.

/9

ميت

خنثى (ابن)	بنت	ابن	ابن	ابن
		ع		
2	1	2	2	2

Chapter 17: Missing Person [المَفْقُود]

A missing person (***mafqūd)*** is the individual whose condition is not known whether he is alive or not. Until his death is confirmed or the judge passes a decision of his death (i.e., after four years, adopted from the Mālikī position), he is to be considered a living person in terms of his own wealth and the rights of his spouse. In terms of other people, he is to be considered a dead person. His share will be suspended like that of the unborn child.

Apply the same method as the Unborn Child (Lesson 15), calculating the *taṣḥiḥ* twice, firstly assuming him to be living and then dead.

Example 17.1.

A woman is survived by her husband, two sisters and a brother who is missing. Calculate the shares which must be given to the heirs immediately.

Assuming life.

			/56
7			/8
مضروب: 4			/2
ميت			
أخ (حيّ)	أخت	أخت	زوج
	ع		½
	1		1
2	1	1	4
14	7	7	28

Assuming death.

/56

مضروب: 8 /6 → /7

ميـــــت

أخ (ميّت)	أخت	أخت	زوج
0		⅔	½
0	2	2	3
0	16	16	24*

* The underlined shares are distributed immediately. Upon confirming the state of the *mafqūd*, the suspended amount will be returned to the remaining heirs.

Chapter 18: Prisoner [الأَسِيْر], Apostate [المُرْتَد] and Simultaneous Deaths

Prisoner: A Muslim, imprisoned by disbelievers, will be deserving of his inheritance as long as he is alive. If there is no news regarding whether he is alive, the laws of *mafqūd* will apply. If he apostates or leaves the fold of Islam, the laws of *murtad* will apply.

Apostate: If a Muslim, Allah forbid, apostates and passes away in this state or the judge passes a decision that he is linked with *Dār al-Ḥarb*, the wealth he owned as a Muslim will be distributed amidst his heirs. However, if he repents and becomes a Muslim, then he will renew his marriage contract and remain the owner of his wealth. However, the wealth that he earned in *irtad* will go to *Bayt al-Māl*. If he flees to *Dār al-Ḥarb*, whatever wealth he earns will be distributed amongst the Muslims like booty.

Simultaneous Deaths: A number of relatives pass away together, by drowning in a river, being burnt, etc. and it is not known who passed away first.

In the case of simultaneous deaths, the link between the inheritors will be considered as non-existent. This means they will not be in a position where they can be classified as recipients of inheritance from each other. The inheritance of the relatives is calculated separately.

Glossary

Amah [أَمَة] - The complete female slave.

al-Aḥyā' [الْأَحْيَاء] - The living heirs of the one inherited from.

'Aṣabah [عَصَبَة] - Residuaries. The heirs with **no** stipulated share in the estate. They inherit the remainder of the estate along with the heirs with a stipulated share or all of the estate, if alone.

'Aṣabah bi Ghayrihi [عَصَبَة بِغَيْرِه] - The female heir who, in the presence of her brother, will get half of his share.

'Aṣabah bi Nafsihi [عَصَبَة بِنَفْسِه] - The male heir that is linked to the deceased directly, like a son or indirectly, like a grandson.

'Aṣabah ma'a Ghayrihī [عَصَبَة مَع غَيْرِه] - The full or consanguine sisters of the deceased that are included in the estate along with the daughter or granddaughter of the deceased.

'Aṣabah Nasabī [عَصَبَة نَسَبِي] - The heirs that are linked to the deceased by way of lineage or family, like father or son.

'Aṣabah Sababī [عَصَبَة سَبَبِي] - The heirs that are linked to the deceased by way of ownership and emancipation, like a master who freed the deceased.

'Awl [عَوْل] - The increase of the lowest common denominator (LCD) to include all of the shares.

Awlād [أَوْلَاد] - The immediate children or male descendents.

Bayt al-Māl [بَيْتُ الْمَال] - Islamic treasury.

Dayn [دَيْن] - Debt.

Dhawu al-Arḥām [ذَوُو الْأَرْحَام] - The heir that is linked to the deceased through a female, like maternal grandfather, maternal uncle or maternal grandchild.

Dhawu al-furūḍ [ذَوُو الْفُرُوْض] - Inheritors with Stipulated Shares. The heirs with a stipulated share in the estate based on the Quran.

Farīq [فَرِيق] - A group of inheritors

Ḥajab [الحجب] - The prevention of certain individuals from inheriting in the presence of a more deserving heir.

Ḥajab Ḥirmān [حَجَب حِرْمَان] - The method of complete deprivation in the presence of a more deserving heir, such as the son preventing the grandson.

Ḥajab Nuqṣān [حَجَب نُقْصَان] - The method of partial deprivation in the presence of a more deserving heir, such as the wife's share being reduced in the presence of children

'Ilm al-farā'id [عِلْم الْفَرَائِض] - The Science of Inheritance Distribution. The knowledge of jurisprudence laws and subsidiary rulings, through which the method of dividing the estate of the deceased amongst its rightful heirs is recognized.

Jadd Fāsid [جَدّ فَاسِد] - The maternal grandfather who is linked to the deceased through a female, maternal grandfather or the maternal grandfather of the father.

Jaddah Fāsidah [جَدّة فَاسِدَة] - The mother's paternal grandmother or paternal grandmother's paternal grandmother who is linked to the deceased in such a way that a maternal grandfather (Jadd Fāsid) does not come in between.

Jadd Ṣaḥīḥ [جَدّ صَحِيْح] - The paternal grandfather who is linked to the deceased in such a way that no female relative comes in between them.

Jaddah Ṣaḥīḥah [جَدّة صَحِيْحَة] - The paternal and maternal grandmother who is linked to the deceased in such a way that no maternal grandfather (Jadd Fāsid) that comes in between, like maternal great-grandfather or maternal great-grandmother.

al-Mablagh [الْمَبْلَغ] - The last number of increased shares after a series of heirs have passed away before the estate was distributed.

Mā fī al-yad [مَا فِي الْيَد] - The inherited share of a deceased that he received from an ascendent.

Maḥjūb [مَحْجُوْب] - The deprived heir.

Maḥrūm [مَحْرُوْم] - The heir who is deprived of inheritance when the means of deprivation are found, like a disbelieving son.

Makhraj/Makhārij [مَخَارِج/مَخرج] - The lowest common denominator (LCD).

Man Lā Yuradd [مَنْ لا يُرَدّ] - The heirs that are **not** included in the redistribution of the estate, like the spouses.

Man Yuradd [مَنْ يُرَدّ] - The heirs that are included in the redistribution of the estate, like the father.

Mawāni'u al-Irth[مَوانِعُ الْإِرْث] - The means of preventing an heir from inheriting, like slavery, murder, differences in religion or country and confusion about the deceased.

Mawlā al-Muwālāt [مَوْلَى الْمُوالَاة] - The one who made the contract of clientage with another.

Mudabbar/ Mudabbarah [مُدبَّر / مُدبَّرَة] - The male or female slave who is promised freedom after the master's death.

Mukātab/ Mukātabah [مُكَاتَب/ مُكَاتَبَة] - The male or female slave who contracts his emancipation in exchange for a specific monetary amount.

Munāsakhah [مُنَاسَخَة] - The redistribution of an heir's share when he dies before receiving it.

Muqar lahu bi-Nasab 'alā Ghayrihī [مُقَر لَهُ بِالنَسَبِ عَلَى غَيْرِهِ] - The confession of a family link in which one does not become part of the lineage, like one confessing that so-and-so is his brother.

Muqar lahu bi-Nasab 'alā Nafsihī [مُقَر لَهُ بِالنَسَبِ عَلَى نَفْسِهِ] - The confession of a family link in which one becomes part of the lineage, like one confessing that so-and-so is his father.

Muqāsamat al-Jadd [مُقَاسَمَتُ الْجَدّ] - The inclusion of the grandfather as a brother in the estate.

Mūrith a'lā [مورِث اعلى] - The first person to pass away in multiple generations of inheritors.

Mūṣā bihi [مُوْصَى بِه] - The item bequeathed.

Mūṣā lahu [مُوْصَى لَه] - The one for whom the bequest is made.

Mūṣī [مُوْصِي] - The one who makes a bequest.

Mu'taq [مُعْتَق] - The slave who is freed.

Mu'tiq [مُعْتِق] - The one who frees a slave.

Muwālāt [مُوَالَاة] - A pact of mutual contract of clientage between two individuals.

Qinn [قِنّ] - The complete male slave.

Radd [رَدّ] - The redistribution of the estate after the stipulated shares.

Ra's/ Ru'ūs [رَأْس/رُؤُوْس] - The group of heirs amongst whom the shares are divided.

Sahm/ Sihām [سَهْم/ سِهَام] - The legislated share of an heir.

Ṣinf [صِنْف] - The heirs in a group with the same general quality, like father, paternal grandfather, etc.

Tabāyun [تبَايُن] - Two numbers having only 1 as a common factor, like 3 and 7.

Tadākhul [تَدَاخُل] - Two numbers having multiple common factors, like 8 and 16.

Ṭā'ifa [طَائِفَة] - A group of heirs having the same link to the deceased, like daughters and grandmothers.

Takhāruj [تَخَارُج] - Settlement of an heir's share for an agreed commodity.

Tamāthul [تَمَاثُل] - Two numbers are the same, like 3 and 3.

Tarikah [تَرِكَة] - Estate. The possessions (real or in debt) that a deceased leaves behind.

Taṣḥīḥ [تَصْحِيح] - The increase of the shares proportionally when they cannot be equally divided amongst the heirs, to avoid decimals.

Tawāfuq [تَوَافُق] - Two numbers having one common factor besides 1, like 3 and 9.

References

Ibn Abd al-Barr, Abu 'Umar Yusuf ibn Abdullah. *al-Istī'āb fī ma'rifat al-aṣḥāb*. 4 vols. Dar al-Jeel, Amman: 1412/1992.

Abdur-Rasheed, Muhammad al-Sajawandi. *al-Sirājī fī al-mīrāth ma' ḥāshiyah dalīl al-wārith*. Al-Bushra Publishers, Karachi: 1432/2011.

Abu Dawud, Sulayman bin Ash'ath. *Sunan Abu Dawud.* Darussalam, New York: 1428/2008.

Ibn Majah, Muhammad bin Yazid al-Qazwini. *Sunan ibn Majah*. Darussalam, New York: 1428/2007.

Hasan, Mahmood. *Mu'īn al-Farā'iḍ*. Jamiah Husainiyah Rander, Surat: 1392/1972.

al-Haskafi, 'Ala ad-deen Muhammad ibn 'Ali. *al-Durr al-Mukhtār*. Dar al-kutub al-'ilmiyya, Beirut: 1423/2002.

Moolla, Abdullah. *Islamic Heir & Distribution.* Jamiah Husainiyah Rander, Surat: 1438/2017.

Nuwiwala, Muhammad Usman. *Asaan Meerath.* Idaarat al-Saeed, Karachi: 1431/2010.

South Africa, Majlisul Ulama. *Kitaabul Meerath: The Book of Inheritance.* Young Men's Muslim Association, Benoni.

Made in the USA
Monee, IL
02 November 2026

67380859R00044